Soul of Detroit

A GUIDE TO EXCEPTIONAL EXPERIENCES

WRITTEN BY MARGOT GUICHETEAU

JONGLEZ PUBLISHING

Travel guides

CREDIT
SIMMONS AND CLARK
JEWELERS
BULOVA WATCHES
BULOVA
Detroit
BEER Co
EST. 2003 · DETROIT, MICHIGAN
SCHOOL
IRONS
AND

“THERE IS A RESILIENCE
THAT RISES FROM SOMEWHERE
DEEP WITHIN YOUR STREETS”

EMINEM - ***LETTER TO DETROIT***

Passionate about Detroit, her Polish maternal family's hometown, Parisian journalist Margot Guicheteau traded Paris for the Motor City. She built a striking, cutting-edge home in Core City, one of Detroit's up-and-coming neighborhoods. As president of the local community association, she works hand-in-hand with city officials on revitalization efforts. Always on the lookout for the next great discovery, she crisscrosses Detroit in search of its hidden gems and off-the-beaten-path treasures.

Detroit isn't easy to grasp at first. The scars of its unprecedented economic collapse are still visible, standing alongside remnants of its storied past—a past that once made Detroit one of America's most vital cities. Through it all, Detroit has stayed true to its core: resilient, authentic, and surprisingly elegant.

This sprawling city features renovated neighborhoods that exist as islands of revival, connected by areas that are still finding their way. Newcomers often struggle to navigate it all. You need to venture beyond the surface, push through a few doors to truly understand Detroit and discover its hidden identity.

Then suddenly, the Motor City reveals itself – standing proud of its heritage while moving forward without compromising its soul. Here, locals never tire of discussing their hometown; it's woven into the very being of the residents who rescued it, reimagined it, and gave it new life. Detroit isn't just a city – it's a daily source of inspiration and endless possibility.

WHAT YOU WON'T FIND IN THIS GUIDE

- Urban exploration sites to photograph
- Urban farms
- A list of the renowned artists exhibited at the Detroit Institute of Art

WHAT YOU WILL FIND IN THIS GUIDE

- Authentically Detroit chocolates
- A bar where you can try feather bowling
- An Orthodox church where you can eat beef Stroganoff
- A hidden club in the basement of a half-abandoned old hotel
- Hare Krishna disciples
- A Russian *banya* unlike any you've seen before

SYMBOLS USED IN **SOUL OF DETROIT**

Under
$20

Quintessential
Detroit

Totally
underground

Historic
site

Accessible
by car

Opening times often vary,
so we recommend checking them directly
on the website of the place you plan to visit.

30 EXPERIENCES

01. Coffee shop by day, intimate techno club by night
02. A truly underground club
03. Search for a treasure in a massive used bookstore
04. A karaoke experience like no other
05. The best jazz, blues, and Motown in town
06. The world's largest Masonic temple
07. A coffee shop for intellectuals and music lovers
08. Taste the chocolates at Bon Bon B
09. Take a figure-drawing class in a private club
10. Exploring the experimental Core City
11. Soul food on a vacant lot
12. Indulge in a burnt Basque-style cheesecake
13. Eat like you're in El Salvador
14. Three one-of-a-kind movie theate
15. A futuristic playground

6. A museum honoring the power of African traditions
7. A yoga class followed by a delicious broth
8. Get whipped with oak leaves in a sauna
9. Dabble in *magick* at a bar like no other
0. The best places for fish
. Amazing gardens created in formerly abandoned lots

22. Taste Lisa Ludwinski's pies
23. The hottest beer in town
24. Discover the secrets of Belle Isle
25. Eat, meditate, and practice yoga in a Hare Krishna temple
26. Surprising flavors on the waterfront
27. Try feather bowling with Belgians
28. Step back in time to 1930s Germany
29. The most iconic donuts in the city
30. Spend some quality time in the suburbs

PHOTOS © SPKRBOX / JEFF HAGE

#01

COFFEE SHOP BY DAY, INTIMATE TECHNO CLUB BY NIGHT

Located in downtown, at the corner of Grand River Avenue and Griswold Street, is a small building made entirely of glass and orange panels from the 1960s. The venue has managed to retain its psychedelic vibe, even though the dark wood walls, small octagonal tables, and orange leather bar have been updated over time.

SPKRBOX
200 GRAND RIVER AVE

(313) 496-1010

spkrbox.bar
Instagram: @spkrbox.detroit

Long and narrow, this intimate spot can only fit a limited number of people, but you'll always find a cozy corner to settle into.

At the bar, the cocktails (El Duderino is a favorite) feature coffee as their base. Once you've placed your order, head upstairs to catch the current DJ spinning. The space is just as small, but the experience is truly worth it, especially with the downtown view and the immersive techno beats.

At 10pm, head downstairs. For just $10, you can hear the best sounds in the city, even on weekdays.

#02

A TRULY **UNDERGROUND CLUB**

For a genuine underground experience in Detroit, head to Leland City Club: enter from Bagley Street, then climb the main wooden staircase to reach the former ballroom entrance of what was once the Leland Hotel.

The place reflects the splendor of yesteryear: peeling paint and moldings and chandeliers from another era recall the building's glory days.

Then descend into the club with its industrial and gothic atmosphere: black concrete walls covered in graffiti, people wearing dramatic makeup and edgy outfits.

The Goth Nights are the most renowned events but keep an eye on the schedule for techno parties that run until 4 in the morning.

LELAND CITY CLUB
400 BAGLEY ST

(313) 962-2300

lelandcityclub.net
Instagram: @lelandcityclub

CLUB

© DAN GAKEN

© DAN GAKEN

#03

SEARCH FOR A TREASURE IN A MASSIVE USED BOOKSTORE

"Do you need help?" the employees will always ask, walkie-talkie in hand, while offering you a map to help you better navigate. Nobody really knows how to approach this place.

In this former glove factory, five floors are filled with used books, all collected by the owner, John K. King.

It's always advisable to have at least some idea of the book category you're looking for, as the place is packed with treasures of all kinds.

The owner himself has found a few gems over the years: an original photo of Mark Twain slipped inside the cover of one of his books and a 1950s pamphlet signed by John F. Kennedy.

JOHN K. KING USED & RARE BOOKS
901 W LAFAYETTE BLVD

(313) 961-0622

johnkingbooksdetroit.com
Instagram: @johnkingbooksdetroit

#04

A KARAOKE EXPERIENCE LIKE NO OTHER

Paul Devitt embodies the New York spirit: a strong accent, a laid-back walk, humor, and, above all, overflowing creativity. What he loves most are bar concepts. In New York, he became famous with the Beauty Bar, a unique spot where you could order a cocktail while getting your nails done. But once others started copying the idea, Paul wanted to reinvent himself. So he decided to open a piano-bar karaoke in New York, Nashville, and Detroit.

In a small alley in downtown Motor City, the success was immediate. The bar is packed nearly every night, from Wednesday to Saturday. To find the entrance, just follow the simple, sleek Sid Gold's neon sign. Once you step inside, a completely different atmosphere welcomes you: a décor that blends Mid-Century style with vintage touches, accompanied by the classics of a karaoke session in the background.

SID GOLD'S REQUEST ROOM
1511 BROADWAY ST

(313) 631-3526

sidgolds.com
Instagram: @sidgolds

© SID GOLD'S REQUEST ROOM

When Paul is in Detroit, he loves to grab the mic and ignite the crowd in the back room, under a ceiling decorated with clouds and swirling galaxy motifs, painted by New York artist Steven Hammel.

His favorite song? "Suspicious Minds" by Elvis Presley.

Guests can choose their favorite songs by scanning a QR code that leads to a carefully curated list by the artists – three pianists who rotate every month.

And if you're lucky, you might catch David Ruffin Jr., the son of David Ruffin, one of the legendary Temptations singers.

#05

THE BEST
JAZZ, BLUES, AND MOTOWN IN TOWN

When Berry Gordy launched his Motown label in 1959, no one could have predicted the monumental impact it would have on the music world. A few iconic bars in Detroit continue to uphold this incredible legacy.

> **Raven Lounge:** Nestled in the heart of Poletown, a neighborhood once home to a Polish community and now somewhat deserted, stands one of the few bars still in operation: the Raven Lounge. Here, locals mix with younger crowds for a laid-back, grunge-style vibe.

> **Baker's:** People come here for the authenticity and to imagine the days when Nat King Cole would sit at the piano or when Ella Fitzgerald, passing through town, would stop by to sing with Tommy Flanagan.

RAVEN LOUNGE
5145 CHENE ST

(313) 924-7133

Facebook: The Raven Lounge

RAVEN LOUNGE

BAKER'S KEYBOARD LOUNGE

© VALERIE SAMSON

BAKER'S KEYBOARD LOUNGE
20510 LIVERNOIS

(313) 345-6300

bakerskeyboardloungedet.com
Instagram: @bakerskeyboardlounge

CLIFF BELL'S

CLIFF BELL'S
2030 PARK AVE

(313) 961-2543

cliffbells.com
Instagram: @cliffbells

CLIFF BELL'S

© TOM HAGERTY

> **Cliff Bell's:** For an elegant night out, head to Cliff Bell's. This chic club draws professionals who come to participate in jam sessions throughout the evening. The refined décor, featuring bronze and mahogany, is highlighted by a mural that stretches across the room, depicting playful cats fishing in an aquatic garden. The piece was inspired by the bar's former doorman, Roosevelt Callen, known as Rosie, who rescued many cats from the building next door.

> **Bert's:** Located in the heart of Eastern Market, Bert's is the place where the crowd dances to the sounds of Motown, jazz, blues, and even improvisation, especially on weekends during market days. The outdoor barbecue adds to the experience. It's a must-visit spot for anyone looking to dance and enjoy a good time.

BERT'S MARKET PLACE
2727 RUSSELL ST

(313) 567-2030 | bertsentertainmentcomplex.squarespace.com

PARKING

#06

THE WORLD'S LARGEST **MASONIC TEMPLE**

Rescued from bankruptcy in 2022 when rock star Jack White stepped in to pay off its $142,000 debt, Detroit's Masonic Temple stands as the largest Masonic building in the world.

This architectural masterpiece now hosts concerts and film productions, and opens to the public once a month for a two-hour guided tour (check the website for dates).

MASONIC TEMPLE
500 TEMPLE ST

(313) 832-7100

themasonic.com
Instagram: @masonicdet

© JEFF WHITE 2004

The stunning 14-story structure contains 26 Masonic lodges, a chapel, two theaters, two ballrooms, and a famous abandoned swimming pool that was never completed due to the Great Depression. Instead of swimmers, the unfinished pool occasionally served as a training pit for the lions and tigers of the Shrine Circus.

More recently, Eminem filmed his music video *Guts Over Fear* here.

MAGNA · EST · VERITAS

#07

A COFFEE SHOP FOR **INTELLECTUALS AND MUSIC LOVERS**

Of all the cafes in Detroit, Trinosophes undoubtedly stands out for its alternative and intellectual atmosphere.

For its owners, Joel Peterson (composer) and Rebecca Mazzei (editor, poet, and art exhibition curator), this place is much more than just a cafe: it's a genuine platform for independent musicians, an incubator for ideas, discussions and exhibitions.

Each week, concerts take place in the adjacent room where Joel and Rebecca prioritize musical quality above all, regardless of genre.

TRINOSOPHES
1464 GRATIOT AVE

(313) 778-9258

trinosophes.com
Instagram: @trinosophes et @cafe.trinosophes

© TRINOSOPHES (INSTAGRAM)

For those who simply want to enjoy the space, Trinosophes offers a menu of sandwiches, quiches, salads, soups, and homemade desserts prepared by a team composed exclusively of artists. Everything here is vegan and gluten-free. Don't miss their chai – it hits the perfect balance of spices and packs some serious flavor.

© DAN DIRITO PHOTOGRAPHY

© TRINOSOPHES (INSTAGRAM)

BON
SPRINKLE POP
CAN-O-CHOCOLATE COVERED COFFEE BEANS
CAN-O-CHOCOLATE COVERED CACAO BEANS
WHITE CHOCOLATE
PENCILS
WOKE UP BON AS HELL AGAIN MUG

1
PICK YOUR BONS
BON BON BON

#08

TASTE THE CHOCOLATES AT BON BON BON

In Midtown, a must-visit is Bon Bon Bon, chocolates 100% "made in Detroit." Alexandra Clark, the founder, is a success story in her own right.

In a pink setting, the sellers (mostly women), dressed in their blue jumpsuits with their names sewn in pink, welcome you with their biggest smiles.

Their outfits recall the origins of the Motor City, a car manufacturing town, where blue-collar culture has become a strength.

BON BON BON
441 W CANFIELD ST SUITE 12

(313) 316-1430

bonbonbon.com
Instagram: @bonbonbonchocolate

The entire setting is very "Willy Wonka-esque" and it's important for Alexandra to show what goes on behind the scenes. The key to her success lies in her honesty and a willingness to work hard.

Shopping here is an experience in itself. The selection is diverse, and the flavors are intriguing: strawberry and balsamic vinegar, Earl Grey tea, crème brûlée, chili and paprika infusion, coffee and donuts. Once selected, each treat is carefully placed in a double-walled cardboard box – material more commonly used in the auto industry. In fact, the packaging has become the brand's signature – a marketing asset entirely imagined by Alexandra.

You'll also discover the three Bons that change frequently: one for the season, one for the month, and one for the current zodiac sign.

Add to that the five collections of the year, and you'll have the complete range of surprising flavors created by Alexandra Clark.

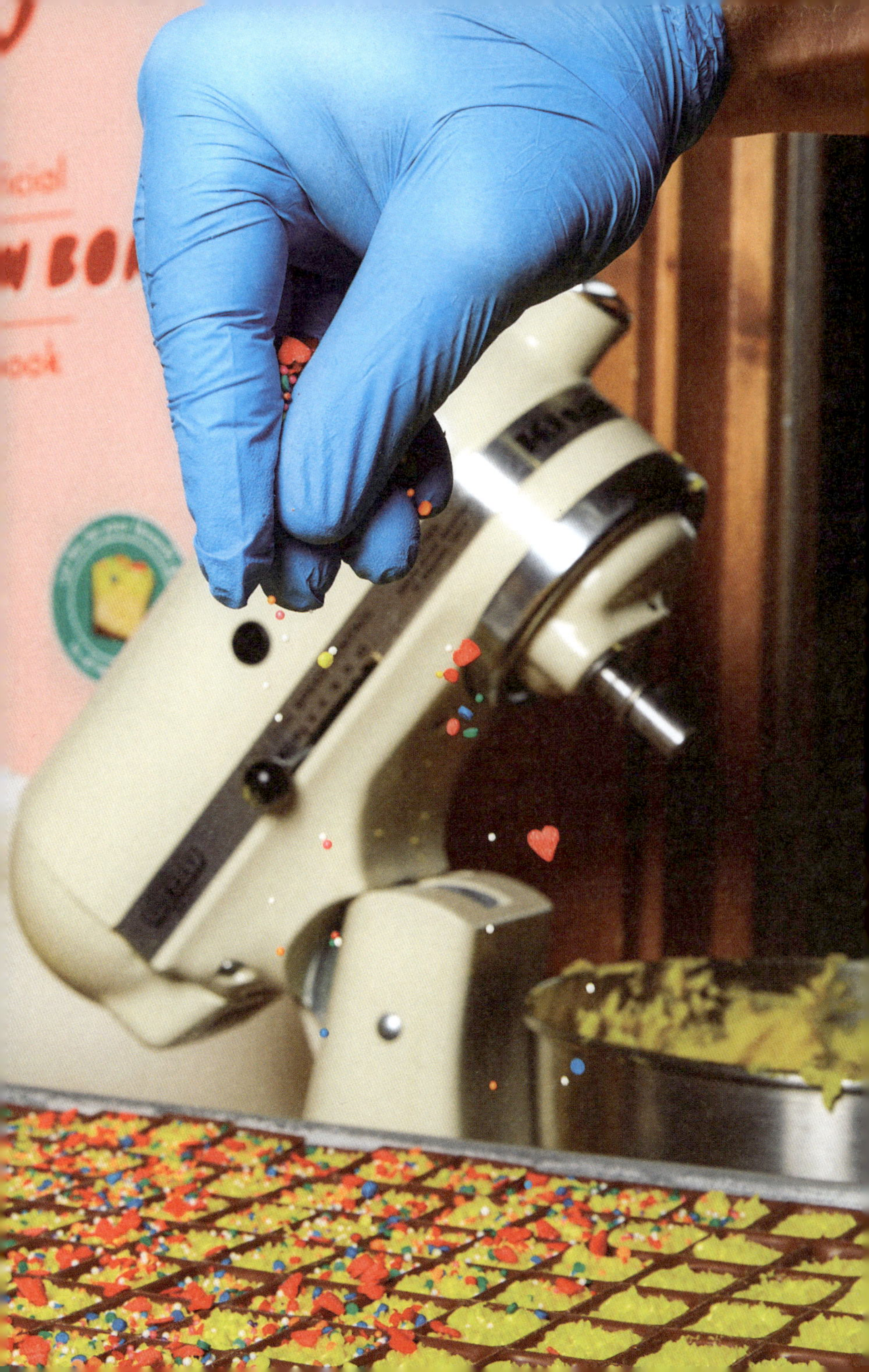

#09

TAKE A FIGURE- DRAWING CLASS IN A PRIVATE CLUB

While many clubs are still active in Detroit, they're typically quite elitist and require membership.

Founded in 1907 by a group of artists and patrons, the Scarab Club opens to the public for certain events that allow you to discover this intimate venue. For $15, for example, you can take a figure-drawing class with a live model.

After class, take some time to explore the place with its medieval-influenced decor, all in dark wood, and its beautiful frescoes and paintings.

The club's greatest pride is the famous beam on the second floor, where many artists have signed their names: Diego Rivera, Marcel Duchamp, Margaret Bourke-White, Isamu Noguchi ...

SCARAB CLUB
217 FARNSWORTH ST

(313) 306-9191

scarabclub.org
Instagram: @scarabclubdetroit

Clarence H. Carter
John Sloan
Max Eastman

#10

EXPLORING THE EXPERIMENTAL **CORE CITY**

Core City stands out as Detroit's most cutting-edge neighborhood and has become the go-to spot for architects and designers.

Investor Philip Kafka, who made his fortune in New York's advertising world, embarked on a completely different adventure about ten years ago: revitalizing a near-deserted neighborhood close to downtown.

His vision is simple: each place he creates is an experience in itself, surrounded by nature. His first project – metal huts – brings a futuristic vision. Further on, a long metal building divided into eight apartments is even more surprising. The ceilings are almost as high as in a cathedral, and the place is protected by a small dense forest.

Today, New Yorkers, Canadians, and even some French have decided to build homes in this buzzing neighborhood.

© CAFE PRINCE

To start your walk, head to Core City Park where you can grab a coffee at **Cafe Prince**, have a bagel at **Bev's Bagels** and, on weekends, taste the best bread in the city at the next-door bakery, **Mother Loaf**.

CAFE PRINCE **4884 GRAND RIVER AVE, UNIT 1A**	**BEV'S BAGELS** **4884 GRAND RIVER AVE**
thecafeprince.com Instagram: @cafeprince.corecity	bevsbagels.com Instagram: @bevsbagels

THE MOTHER LOAF BREAD
4884 GRAND RIVER BLVD

(313) 512-8292

Instagram: @themotherloaf

On 18th Street, a community garden and wooden structures house the **Huckleberry Explorers Club Museum**. A couple of intellectuals have chosen to live outside the mainstream there. Stefany Ann Golberg (better known as Shuffy) is a Buddhist, and her partner, Morgan Meis, is a Franciscan. After living in Brooklyn for many years, they decided to create their own fantasy universe. Their house has a general store, a small thrift shop where Shuffy sells whatever comes to mind and has fun writing a little message for each object. In the other room, the walls are covered with cardboard hiding small messages and objects. Grab one of the magnifying glasses provided to take a closer look and let yourself be inspired by the poetry of this room.

HUCKLEBERRY EXPLORERS CLUB MUSEUM
2660 BUCHANAN ST

huckleberryclub.com

For dinner, you'll have several options: **Barda**, a restaurant with Argentine influences; **Puma**, its annex, which offers delicious sandwiches, like *choripan* (spicy Argentine sausage), at more reasonable prices; **Lady of the House** for a farm-to-table experience; and Vesper, a wine bar set up in a former bank where you can enjoy reading one of the excellent cookbooks, all available for purchase.

End the night in one of the neighborhood's Airbnbs and you'll have had an exceptional day!

DA

A

BARDA

© BARDA

BARDA
4842 GRAND RIVER AVE

(313) 952-5182

bardadetroit.com
Instagram: @barda_detroit

PUMA

PUMA
4725 16TH ST

(313) 819-6804

pumadetroit.com
Instagram: @puma_detroit

LADY OF THE HOUSE
4884 GRAND RIVER AVE UNIT 1C

(313) 230-4678
ladyofthehousedetroit.com
Instagram: @ladyofthehousedetroit

VESPER BOOKS & WINE
5001 GRAND RIVER AVE

(313) 716-1708
vesperbooksandwine.com
Instagram: @vesperbooksandwine

#11

SOUL FOOD
ON A VACANT LOT

Every Thursday from May to October for the past decade, Chef Meiko Krishok and her Pink Flamingo pop-up team take over a vacant lot in North Corktown. Here, they serve up dishes with explosive flavors – often Asian-inspired with Soul Food influences – using ingredients from surrounding farms.

Bring family, friends, or neighbors and unwind at a picnic table or lounge on the garden's oversized pink tires.

On the menu, you'll always find a vegetarian dish and a meat-based dish, three iconic sauces (banana ketchup, chipotle miso, herb sauce), hibiscus lemonade, and the famous rice balls, inspired by Meiko's grandmother's recipe. A truly unique experience!

PINK FLAMINGO
CORKTOWN POP-UP
2746 VERMONT ST

Every Thursday from May to October	(313) - 826-1454	pinkflamingodetroit.com Instagram: @pinkflamingodetroit

PHOTOS © BRITTANY GREESON

OPEN

GREEN SAUCE
BANANA KETCHUP

PHOTOS © GERARD + BELEVENDER

#12

INDULGE **IN A BURNT BASQUE-STYLE CHEESECAKE**

Housed in a former firehouse from 1910, Ladder 4 attracts both trendy Detroit locals and upscale suburban diners seeking a refined, classic dining experience.

The dishes here are always perfectly balanced, with surprising and creative twists on familiar favorites. Chef John Yelinek doubles as the restaurant's sommelier, curating a selection of hard-to-find European wines rarely available elsewhere in the States.

If you don't have time for a full meal, don't miss their signature burnt Basque-style cheesecake, drizzled with a vinegar reduction, and take the opportunity to pair it with a glass of wine.

LADDER 4 WINE BAR
3396 VINEWOOD ST

(313) 638-1601

ladder4winebar.com
Instagram: @ladder4winebar

BIG MOOD

#13

EAT LIKE **YOU'RE IN EL SALVADOR**

In Southwest Detroit's Hispanic neighborhood, hidden among countless food trucks and restaurants, there's a *pupusería* on Livernois Avenue that deserves a visit.

The place doesn't look like much, but that's part of its charm: napkins hung on the walls like paintings illustrate Salvadoran traditions and set the tone. Here, hardly anyone speaks English and nearly all the customers are Hispanic.

For $3, you can order the national dish, a *pupusa* – a Salvadoran flatbread made from corn meal or rice flour, similar to Venezuelan and Colombian *arepas*, stuffed with cheese, meat, vegetables ... The dish comes with fermented cabbage and spicy sauces. And don't miss the perfectly cooked plantains, soft and caramelized, served with cream and a salty, spicy bean purée.

PUPUSERÍA Y RESTAURANTE SALVADOREÑO
3149 LIVERNOIS

(313) 899-4020

© MYTHY HUYNH

El Salvador
PUPUSAS
DE QUESO,
ARROZ Y
CHICHARRÓN
-TAMALES
-CAFE

PHOTOS © HELMUT ZIEWERS

#14

THREE ONE-OF-A-KIND **MOVIE THEATERS**

To the delight of film buffs, Detroit is home to three movie theaters with unique architecture and carefully curated programming.

> **Redford Theatre**

Have you ever seen a 1928 theater decorated like a Japanese temple? Welcome to the Redford Theatre, a truly fantastic world. Come rediscover cinema classics with family or friends and keep an eye on their schedule.

A silent film accompanied by a historic organ

At the Redford Theatre and The Senate, silent films are accompanied live by a magnificent organ. At the Redford, the organ is a Barton, majestically installed on stage. It's an instrument of exceptional rarity, maintained by the Motor City Theatre Organ Society.

REDFORD THEATRE
17360 LAHSER RD

(313) 537-2560

redfordtheatre.com
Instagram: @redfordtheatre

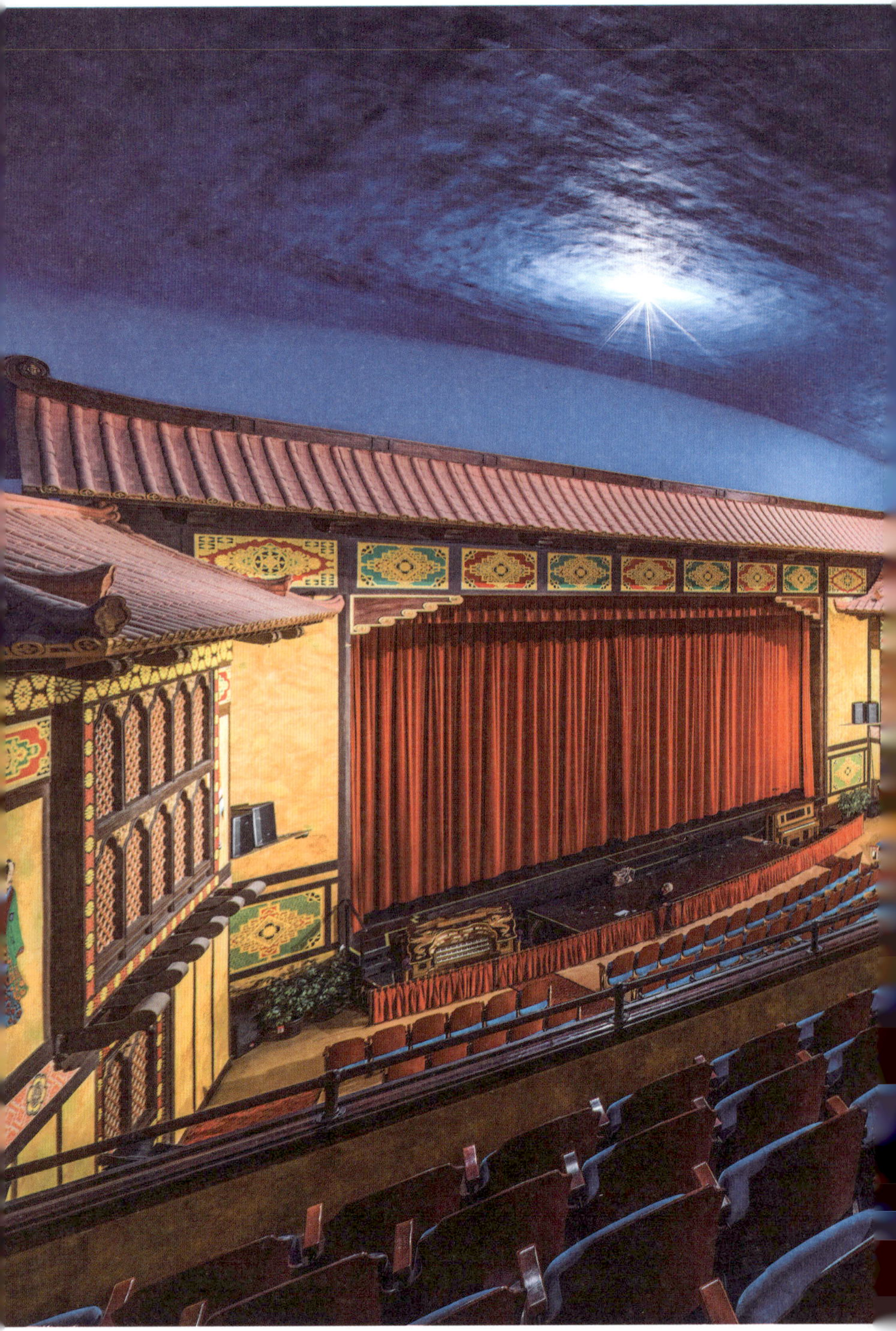

© HELMUT ZIEWERS

> The Senate

Run by the same organization as the Redford Theatre, The Senate has endured hardships but has stood the test of time. Though its architecture is more subdued than its counterpart's, a few Art Deco touches give it a unique charm. Its more specialized and alternative programming particularly appeals to the city's young creatives.

SENATE THEATER
2957, 6424 MICHIGAN AVE

(313) 894-0850

senatetheater.com
Instagram: @senatetheater

> The DFT

In the heart of the DIA (Detroit Institute of Arts), Detroit's major art museum, sits a magnificent theater, the DFT (Detroit Film Theatre). People come for its quality programming that changes weekly. Elliot Wilhelm, the programming director, travels the world throughout the year to select the films he wants to show. Film enthusiasts also love to attend the short film festival, a DFT tradition.

DETROIT FILM THEATRE
5200 JOHN R ST

(313) 833-4005

dia.org/events/detroit-film-theatre
Instagram DIA: @diadetroit

SENATE
Home of the
Detroit Theater
Organ Society
Home of the
Detroit Theater
Organ Society
DTOS
SILENT MOVIE
ORGAN POPS CONCERT
6424

#15

A FUTURISTIC PLAYGROUND

On Warren Avenue, at the border between Detroit and Dearborn (known for its large Middle Eastern population), stands an unexpected metallic structure with futuristic, angular architecture. Surprisingly, this installation is a children's playground located in Warren Gateway Park.

The play structure itself presents a real challenge: several obstacles must be overcome before reaching the top and sliding down the slide.

The goal was to create a multi-sensory and stimulating project, encouraging kids to let loose outdoors.

This installation is part of a much larger project: the Joe Louis Greenway, a 27-mile greenway whose construction began in 2009.

This circular route surrounds Detroit and passes through several neighborhoods, some of which have long been neglected despite their high population density.

WARREN GATEWAY
JOE LOUIS GREENWAY
8034 W WARREN AVE

© CHELSEA IRONS-LIGHT

The goal is to offer a new perspective on the city, provide access to nature and recreation, and reconnect diverse neighborhoods on foot, reflecting Detroit's cultural and historical diversity.

From the river to the outskirts, you'll discover two more "cities within the city": Hamtramck, once home to many Polish immigrants, now predominantly Yemeni and Bangladeshi;

and Highland Park, with a mostly African-American population. It's recommended to start at the Dequindre Cut, an old railway transformed into a promenade, offering a beautiful industrial panorama.

Locals love biking, rollerblading, skateboarding, or strolling with their families to enjoy seasonal activities and admire the murals.

© MBAD AFRICAN BEAD MUSEUM

© MBAD AFRICAN BEAD MUSEUM

#16

A MUSEUM HONORING **THE POWER OF AFRICAN TRADITIONS**

For years, Detroit was the city of DIY and outsider art: artists often created with materials found on the streets and in abandoned places. The project everyone came to see was the Heidelberg Project (an entire neighborhood transformed into art installations, conceived by artist Tyree Guyton with nearby residents).

In the 2000s, Olayami Dabls, an African-American artist, set up shop at the corner of Grand River and West Grand Boulevard. His vision was to create a space dedicated to his community, reconnecting with the richness of his African heritage, far from European colonialism.

MBAD AFRICAN BEAD MUSEUM
6856 VINEWOOD ST

(313) 898-3007

mbad.org
Instagram: @mbadafricanbeadmuseum

© MBAD AFRICAN BEAD SHOP

MBAD AFRICAN BEAD MUSEUM

On his property, he created art installations made of stone, steel, wood (embodying strength and wisdom, as trees are seen as beings with qualities similar to humans) and mirrors (viewed as portals and used by ancestors to repel negative energies and promote reflection).

Today, visitors delight in exploring his bead museum, where thousands of hanging necklaces remind us of the importance of these objects and their healing power. Always there to welcome you with the warmest smile, Olayami will gladly share all the stories related to his culture.

#17

A YOGA CLASS FOLLOWED BY A DELICIOUS BROTH

An industrial city with long, harsh winters still undergoing economic transition, Detroit can be intense. There's nothing better than a brief respite to recharge and take care of yourself.

Lara Rasmussen, a young German who spent many years in New York, was looking for a high-quality yoga class similar to those she had taken in the big city. When she couldn't find anything that truly met her expectations, she decided to open her own studio and offer a luxury yoga and Pilates experience.

The ultimate highlight? The option to order a delicious broth (chicken or beef) after class. There's nothing better after a workout than this precious elixir, rich in collagen, minerals, and amino acids. It helps with muscle recovery, joint and bone health, digestion, immune system function, sleep quality, and also supports beautiful skin and hair.

HOT BONES
2895 E GRAND BLVD

Instagram: @hotbonesdetroit | hotbonesdetroit.com

HOT
BONES

SCHVITZ

#18

GET WHIPPED WITH OAK LEAVES
IN A SAUNA

On Oakland Avenue, in the calm of a revitalized neighborhood, stands a gray building with minimal decoration. There are few clues to what's inside except for a red neon sign marking the entrance to the Schvitz sauna. Cross the threshold and you'll be greeted by a distinctly David Lynch-esque atmosphere, complete with red carpet and a brass doorbell. For $40, you can spend the entire day at the sauna. Just slip on a swimsuit, bathrobe, and cap, then head downstairs to where you'll find the two *banyas* – one dry, one wet.

The vintage white tile and a "1930" date inscribed on the pool's edge tell you about the history of the place. From the Purple Gang criminal mob of the 1920s to its days as a swingers' club, this spot is packed with colorful stories. Today, it's an iconic destination where all generations mingle.

THE SCHVITZ HEALTH CLUB
8295 OAKLAND AVE

(313) 724-8489

schvitzdetroit.com
Instagram: @theschvitz

For the most authentic experience, request a platza session: for 30 minutes, the owner's daughter whips you with oak leaves on the top floor of the sauna – the hottest spot – before guiding you into an ice-cold plunge pool.

After your sauna treatment, head to the upstairs restaurant, still in your robe, for excellent East European-inspired cuisine.

Want something more private? You can book their Airbnb right next door, which of course includes access to a sauna and ice bath.

SHOWER MAY BE
HOT

1930

#19

DABBLE IN *MAGICK* AT A BAR LIKE NO OTHER

The Black Salt Bar is more than just a bar. Here, you can draw tarot cards, enjoy a cocktail that comes with a small pouch containing charms to help make your wishes come true (complete with instructions), and on Sundays, get your fortune told by a card reader for $35.

For Zoey Ashwood, the owner of Black Salt Bar, the idea of hanging out at a bar also means taking time for yourself and practicing a bit of *magick*, a term from paganism that refers to the ritualization of intentions.

THE BLACK SALT
2764 FLORIAN ST,
HAMTRAMCK, MI 48212

Instagram: @theblacksalt_bar

theblacksaltbar.com

© THE BLACK SALT

N'CHIPS

Scotty Simpson's
FISH & CHIPS
313-533-0950

#20

THE BEST PLACES **FOR FISH**

> **Scotty Simpson's Fish & Chips:** While Detroit isn't exactly the seafood and fish capital of the States, three places are worth seeking out. In a neighborhood that has seen better days, a time-capsule diner resembling a fisherman's shack has survived. Harry Barber has worked at Scotty Simpson's since 1966 and is now the owner. He's behind the stove Tuesday through Saturday. Nothing has changed: plastic fish still hang on the walls, the original carpet remains, and those orange and wooden chairs haven't budged.

Without fail, the waitress will ask if it's your first time. If you answer "yes," she'll say enthusiastically: "Great, we'll see you tomorrow then!" They know their fish and chips is an absolute treat. Their secret? Frying the fish in a half-meat, half-vegetable fat. Their coleslaw is fresh and mayo-free. On Fridays, the desserts are homemade.

SCOTTY SIMPSON'S FISH & CHIPS
22200 FENKELL AVE

(313) 533-0950

scottysfishandchips.com

> **Sweetest Heart of Mary:** A few days during Lent, the Sweetest Heart of Mary Church transforms into a restaurant. The place is very popular with families who come to enjoy a big, friendly meal and order fried fish, fried shrimp, or a delicious soup, often a lobster bisque. Take the opportunity to see the breathtaking church interior – just one of many stunning historic churches throughout Detroit.

SWEETEST HEART OF MARY CHURCH
4440 RUSSELL ST

(313) 831-6659
motherofdivinemercy.org/sweetest-heart-of-mary

Call or visit the website to find out the exact dates

> **Baobab Fare:** At Baobab Fare, an East African restaurant, go for the samaki, a traditional fish dish served with rice, plantains, cold corn, and stewed beans.

BAOBAB FARE
6568 WOODWARD AVE SUITE 100

(313) 265-3093

baobabfare.com
Instagram: @baobabfare

#21

AMAZING GARDENS CREATED IN FORMERLY ABANDONED LOTS

Tucked away in Poletown's quiet neighborhood, you'll find some remarkable gardens – all imagined and created by local residents who've formed their own alternative community.

Andrew "Birch" Kemp, co-director of Arboretum Detroit, moved here about two decades ago. With his passion for trees, he saw potential in the abandoned lots where nature was slowly reclaiming space, and made it his mission to replace as much surrounding concrete as possible with greenery.

Since then, through his 14-member association and local partnerships, he has acquired 40 lots from the city that have been transformed into six public parks.

ARBORETUM DETROIT NURSERY
3300 E PALMER ST

Instagram: @arbdetroit | arbdetroit.org

Trees are a source of inspiration and education, a way to reduce pollution in the city, reconnect with the environment, and even heal.

As you stroll between houses, you'll stumble upon these gardens, each with its own distinct character. Begin at Circle Forest, where they've rebuilt an entire ecosystem – hills carefully designed to channel rainwater to trees, and a wooden walkway that leads to a small forest featuring a playful "floor" made of tree-trunk slices for kids.

Walk a bit further and "Birch" will point out his meadows, explaining how they eliminate lawn mowing while preserving the ecological balance. These natural spaces lower temperatures and restore nutrients to the soil, while their tall grasses create a magical setting where birds love to land.

Keep exploring and let the trees and directional signs be your guides. As "Birch" puts it: "This is a place to learn to love trees and forests."

© SISTER PIE

#22

TASTE
LISA LUDWINSKI'S PIES

Buttery, fruity, and creamy, Lisa Ludwinski's pies are truly one-of-a-kind. They strike a perfect balance – indulgent yet somehow light – and feature ingredients sourced exclusively from local producers. Lisa has built more than just a bakery; she's created a community that cares deeply about its environmental impact and treats its employees as partners who share in the profits.

Inspired by what Michigan (the second-largest agricultural state in the U.S.) has to offer, this pastry chef particularly enjoys following the seasons: think cherries in summer, apples in fall, etc. But if there's one pie you simply must try, it's the one that's on the menu year-round – the salted maple pie.

SISTER PIE
8066 KERCHEVAL AVE

(313) 447-5550

sisterpie.com
Instagram: @sisterpiedetroit

#23

THE HOTTEST BEER IN TOWN

Kyle Hunt, the owner of Collect Beer Bar, has a simple slogan: "Focus on simplicity and let people define the space." Mission accomplished: over the years, Collect has become a must-visit spot, first in its cozy Eastern Market location, and now at Little Village, the trendiest spot in town.

Housed in a white brick building with circular glass paving stones, the décor blends minimalism with contemporary design.

COLLECT BEER BAR
9301 KERCHEVAL AVE

Instagram: @collect.beerbar

collect-beerbar.com

The beer selection, updated weekly and sourced from around the world, attracts both regulars and families alike.

In the summer, kids enjoy the pink concrete benches outside while parents soak in the unique vibe of the place. Two events you can't miss: the Survivor show, airing every

Wednesday, still hugely popular in the U.S., and the Celtic football league games.

This program is generally hard to access in the States, so even people from Northern Michigan are motivated to spend the afternoon here.

AQUARIUM

#24

DISCOVER THE SECRETS **OF BELLE ISLE**

You could spend an entire afternoon uncovering the secrets of Detroit's only island, Belle Isle, and see Canada just across the strait. Imagine, during Prohibition, when bootleggers would ride motorcycles across the frozen lake to fetch bottles of alcohol in Canada and bring them back to the speakeasies of the Motor City.

> **The Aquarium:** Dating from 1904, it's the oldest aquarium in the United States and probably one of the most beautiful. The brick building, designed in Beaux-Arts style, was conceived by famous architects Albert Kahn and George D. Mason.

The interior is particularly impressive: the vaulted ceiling, covered with green opaline tiles, creates the illusion of being underwater, immersing visitors in a unique aquatic atmosphere.

Today, this establishment houses one of the finest collections of air-breathing fish ever exhibited, as well as the only known collection of all seven North American pike species.

BELLE ISLE AQUARIUM
3 INSELRUHE AVE

(313) 331-7760

belleisleconservancy.org/bia
Instagram: @belleisleaquarium

© BRANDON PARSONS

> **The Anna Scripps Whitcomb Conservatory:** Beneath this vast glass dome, hundreds of plants flourish. This structure, another masterpiece by Albert Kahn, was inspired by Thomas Jefferson's Monticello home in Virginia. Visitors can discover an impressive collection of orchids, donated in 1955 by Anna Scripps Whitcomb, heiress to the founder of the *Detroit News*, James E. Scripps. The conservatory is divided into five sections: the Palm House, the Tropical House, the Cactus House, a Fern Garden, and the main hall.

ANNA SCRIPPS WHITCOMB CONSERVATORY
4 INSELRUHE AVE

(313) 821-9844

belleisleconservancy.org/anna-scripps-whitcomb-conservatory
Instagram: @belleisleconservancy

DETROIT - CHARLES FALSETTI

> **The walk to Hipster Beach:** In summer, all the young people love going to Hipster Beach, the island's hidden beach, to swim in the strait. The walk starts at the Blue Lagoon Heron Trail and continues toward the lighthouse (the William Livingstone Memorial Lighthouse) before veering left toward different water spots where you can relax. The tall grasses make you forget city life. The walk is well worth your time no matter what season of the year you visit.

> **Piet Oudolf Park:** In 2016, a Detroit gardening club sent a fan letter to garden superstar, Dutch designer Piet Oudolf, a pioneer of the perennial plant movement, in the hope of convincing him to design a park in Detroit.

After contributing to the landscaping of the High Line in New York and the Lurie Garden in Chicago, he agreed to visit the Motor City, and quickly fell in love with it.

After scouting several sites, he ultimately chose Belle Isle. It's the first time a project has been entirely conceived by the landscape architect himself and implemented solely by volunteers who raised funds over several years – a major point of pride for Detroit residents.

As in all his compositions, Oudolf plays with colors, textures, and heights, offering a continuous spectacle regardless of the season. After tireless work by volunteers, the park now invites visitors to discover a meadow, a rain garden, and, at its heart, a harmonious arrangement of flowers and pathways.

OUDOLF GARDEN DETROIT
LOITER WAY &, PICNIC WAY

(313) 474-4700

oudolfgardendetroit.org
Instagram: @oudolfgardendetroit

25

EAT, MEDITATE, AND PRACTICE YOGA IN A HARE KRISHNA TEMPLE

Located in the stunning Fisher Mansion, the Hare Krishna temple is definitely worth a visit. It was purchased in 1975 by Alfred Brush Ford, great-grandson of Henry Ford, and Elisabeth Reuther Dickmeyer, daughter of United Auto Workers president Walter Reuther. Devotees of Krishna themselves, they simply handed it over to the Krishna followers.

The house, which you can freely explore, boasts 50 rooms and blends Moorish, Spanish, and Italian Renaissance styles. The interior is adorned with marble columns, gold and silver moldings, black walnut panels, hand-painted and leather-covered walls, and rosewood floors.

ISKCON DETROIT (INTERNATIONAL SOCIETY FOR KRISHNA CONSCIOUSNESS)
383 LENOX ST

Yoga: Sundays from 4pm to 5pm; followed by a free vegetarian meal

(313) 331-6740
iskcondetroit.com

At prayer times (check the website for details), the word "Hare Krishna" is chanted 108 times, 16 times daily: this form of meditation is said to help clear the mind and focus the spirit on the relationship with Krishna. At noon, a simple

but delicious free vegetarian Indian lunch is served in the basement. On Sundays, starting at 4:15pm, a communal vegetarian meal known as the Sunday Feast is shared in the main hall. There are also yoga sessions from 5pm to 6pm.

© HARSHANTI

CORIANDER KITCHEN
AND FARM

CORIANDER KITCHEN
AND FARM

26

SURPRISING FLAVORS ON THE WATERFRONT

Who would have thought that Detroit's eastside housed canals? It's along the water, in the charming and peaceful Jefferson Chalmers neighborhood, that **Coriander Kitchen** has chosen to set up shop to offer its customers a surprising experience.

Nothing is more pleasant than coming to relax in a charming outdoor garden, facing the canal, to grab a bite and have a drink.

In winter, the view is just as magical when you settle into the heart of the glass atrium, especially on snowy days.

The dishes are prepared using vegetables from owner Gwen Meyer's farm, or through collaborations with local businesses like the Marrow butcher shop. Everything is delicious.

After your meal, head next door to **Detroit River Sports**, where you can rent a kayak for 90 minutes and explore the strait, discovering the city from a whole new perspective.

CORIANDER KITCHEN AND FARM
14601 RIVERSIDE BLVD

(313) 338-9466
corianderkitchenandfarm.com

DETROIT RIVER SPORTS
14601 RIVERSIDE BLVD

(313) 908-0484
detroitriversports.com
Instagram: @detroitriversports

#27

TRY FEATHER BOWLING WITH BELGIANS

Belgian feather bowling at Cadieux Cafe has a similar vibe to pétanque, with comparable rules, but here you roll what looks like a wooden wheel down a curved lane.

Every Thursday from 7pm until as late as midnight, you'll find the men from the hardcore feather bowling league hanging out, beers in hand, celebrating like they never left Belgium. The ladies take over on Wednesday nights with their own league.

Though the ultimate prize is winning the season championship – which earns you a portrait drawn by Jeremy and the prestigious honor of being displayed on the wall – what truly matters here is the camaraderie.

This spot has become home base for Detroit's Belgian community, boasting an impressive beer selection and authentic specialties like mussels and rabbit stew. Once you give it a try, don't be surprised if they start recruiting you for league membership!

CADIEUX CAFE
4300 CADIEUX RD

(313) 882-8560
cadieuxcafe.com
Instagram: @cadieuxcafe

From September to April, the lanes are reserved for competition on Tuesday, Wednesday and Thursday evenings. On other nights, the lanes can be rented by the public (reservations recommended)
Mon & Tue: $35 per hour per lane; Wed-Sun: $55

THE.CADIEUX.BOWLING.CLUB.
DETROIT

PHOTOS © JARRED GUILD

#28

STEP BACK IN TIME
TO 1930S GERMANY

For a journey back in time, head to the Dakota Inn. Nothing has changed here since 1933, when Karl Kurz, a Ford factory worker, decided to buy an old Chinese laundromat to open his own *Rathskeller* (a "city hall basement," a traditional place in Germany where locals gather for drinks after work).

While the joint started with just a few beers and sandwiches for blue-collar workers from nearby factories, the grandson – also named Karl and the current owner – took over in 1986 and focused on traditional German dishes. On the menu: *Bavarian Bratwurst, Schnitzel, Hähnchenfleisch, Knackwurst* ... served by women in traditional attire.

DAKOTA INN
17324 JOHN R. ST

(313) 867-9722

dakota-inn.com

HOFBRÄU
HOFBRÄU

It's for this authentic atmosphere that everyone still hurries to the restaurant today, Thursday through Saturday. Reservations are highly recommended, especially between 6pm and 10pm, when the singer sits at the piano to liven up the place, with everyone joining in.

Two events not to be missed: *Fasching*, the equivalent of Mardi Gras but happening every Saturday in February, and of course, *Oktoberfest*.

#29

THE MOST ICONIC DONUTS IN THE CITY

On the edge of the city along Woodward Avenue, Detroit's grand and legendary thoroughfare, stands one of the city's most emblematic spots: Dutch Girl Donuts.

The pink and blue neon lights and the small image of a Dutch girl in a traditional dress, bonnet, and wooden clogs on the blue awning set the tone. Everything here has remained unchanged since 1947, the year the Timmer family opened the small shop. Back then, Cecelia worked 14 hours a day running the business.

DUTCH GIRL DONUTS
19000 WOODWARD AVE

(313) 826-6005

dutchgirldetroit.com
Instagram: @dutchgirldetroit

PHOTOS © JARRED GUILD

Dutch Girl
DONUTS
19000
So Delicious!
Dutch Girl Donuts
19000 Woodward
EST.1947
OPEN 24 HOURS
6:00 AM TUESDAY
TO
6:00 PM SUNDAY
CLOSED MONDAY

Today, the business has new owners, but everything has remained the same, except for a few machines that had to be renovated or replaced.

Behind the large bulletproof windows[!], a small team works day and night: the donuts are available 24/7 from Tuesday at 6am until Sunday at 6pm, unless they've already sold out.

© JAMES HAEFNER PHOTOGRAPHY

© PD REARICK

#30

SPEND SOME QUALITY TIME IN THE SUBURBS

Detroit is made up of many suburbs, each very different from the others, and it's fun to find must-visit places in them. Here are our top five recommendations.

> **Cranbrook**, the incubator for modern design icons: Bloomfield Hills is Detroit's most upscale suburb, dotted with stunning mansions and home to Cranbrook Academy of Art, a prestigious design institution housed in Victorian-style buildings. While Europe's post-WWI Bauhaus movement was championing functionality and strict formalism, Michigan was developing its own brand of modernism, heavily inspired by craftsmanship.

From the 1930s onward, the biggest names in design came here to study and work: Charles and Ray Eames, Harry Bertoia, Florence Knoll, and the Saarinen family. This movement greatly influenced American estheticism. Today, people come here to see the museums and visit the hidden gardens in the large park.

CRANBROOK ACADEMY OF ART
39221 WOODWARD AVE,
BLOOMFIELD HILLS, MI 48304

(248) 645-3323

cranbrookart.edu
Instagram: @cranbrook_arts

PHOTOS © THE ROYAL EAGLE

> **The Royal Eagle**, a truly unique Russian dining experience: You wouldn't expect to find an Orthodox monastery tucked away on the edge of Detroit—but there it is. In the early 2000s, Archimandrite Pachomy (Belkoff) was given three years to find land on which to build a Russian Orthodox church. At the time, Detroit was deep in decline, with vacant lots everywhere and endless possibilities. That's when he met a Polish couple in Harper Woods who were about to sell their home. He seized the opportunity. And so began a remarkable journey.

Over the years, he gradually acquired the ten surrounding plots – and even a neighboring garage, once run by a local gang. That garage would eventually become The Royal Eagle, a restaurant now helmed by Chef Petr Balcarovsky.

The concept is simple: one dinner a month, and two afternoon teas each week. All proceeds go directly back into the ongoing construction and upkeep of the monastery grounds.

Make sure to book in advance through their website, and dress to impress. The experience is exclusive and refined – but also incredibly warm and welcoming. Surrounded by ornate Russian décor, you'll enjoy traditional dishes that shaped European culinary history, like beef Stroganoff, borscht, and beef Wellington.

THE ROYAL EAGLE
18725 OLD HOMESTEAD DR,
HARPER WOODS, MI 48225

(313) 521-1894

theroyaleagle.net
Instagram: @the_czech_mate_detroit

> **Sharaku,** a taste of home away from home: About 95% of Japanese expats in Detroit work in the auto industry – and when they're craving something familiar, they head to Sharaku. Ask any regular, and they'll tell you: dining here feels just like home.

Chef Suzuki and manager Ken are committed to preserving tradition. Behind the counter, Suzuki – known for his playful smile – keeps guests entertained while skillfully preparing each dish. Over the years, patrons have gifted him a charming collection of Godzilla figurines, proudly on display. He barely speaks a word of English, but his sushi speaks volumes.

Chef Suzuki honed his craft in his hometown of Niigata, in northern Japan. Following the strict tradition, he wasn't even allowed to touch the fish during the first six years of training. And as Ken will tell you, "You'll know it's a real Japanese restaurant if the miso soup comes after the sushi."

SHARAKU
6159 HAGGERTY RD,
WEST BLOOMFIELD TOWNSHIP, MI 48322

(248) 960-1888

sharakuhanzo.com
Instagram: @sharakudetroit

Ask The
BRAIN

ALEXANDER
THE

weighs
645
lbs

H·B·WARNER
THE MARKET OF
VAIN DESIRE
FOOD
PRESENTS
HUMPTY
DUMPTY
SLUSHIE S

> **Marvin's Marvelous Mechanical Museum,** Detroit's most delightfully bizarre arcade: Detroit's full of oddball gems, but this one might take the cake. Tucked inside a suburban strip mall is a wonderfully weird arcade game collection.

In the 1960s, local pharmacist Marvin Yagoda began collecting arcade machines from around the world. Not just any machines, but quirky contraptions: wooden and papier-mâché figures that perform magic tricks, tell your fortune, and put you to the test.

Eventually, Marvin opened a space to share his growing obsession. These days, the museum still draws crowds of all ages—kids and adults alike—who come to play, rack up tickets in hopes of hitting the jackpot, or just snag a few pieces of candy. Classic arcade machines sit alongside cutting-edge games, with something fun tucked into every corner and something for everyone to enjoy.

MARVIN'S MARVELOUS MECHANICAL MUSEUM
6427 ORCHARD LAKE ROAD,
WEST BLOOMFIELD TOWNSHIP, MI 48322

(248) 626-5020 | marvin3m.com

> **Mabel Gray,** one of Detroit's unmissable restaurants: Over the past ten years, new trendy restaurants have opened every year, but few manage to stand out. Among those that do are Selden Standard, of course – but above all, Mabel Gray in Hazel Park, led by chef James Rigato.

For James, it was essential to set up in this small, working-class suburban town, where dive bars are part of the landscape. In his view, American cuisine is like a land without roots, given how young the country is. That's why he travels to five different countries each year to recharge and stay inspired. And it shows in his dishes: Texan, Japanese, and French influences come together seamlessly, creating explosive flavors that are always perfectly balanced.

James's true passion? Champagne. Every year, he travels to France to explore new vineyards. On the menu, there's a two-page section devoted entirely to champagne, with bottles reaching up to $650.

The restaurant is especially known for its $89 eight-course surprise tasting menu. In August, when local farms are buzzing with activity, the menu goes entirely vegan.

MABEL GRAY
23825 JOHN R RD,
HAZEL PARK, MI 48030

(248) 398-4300

mabelgraykitchen.com
Instagram: @mabelgraykitchen

TOP EVENTS YOU

Dally in the Alley (1): Every September since 1977, on the first Saturday after Labor Day, a neighborhood festival has been held in the heart of Midtown, celebrating local art, culture, food, and music. The event is entirely managed by volunteers, without any commercial sponsors.

St. Patrick's Day: On March 17, in the Irish neighborhood of Corktown, a celebration commemorates the death of St. Patrick, Ireland's patron saint. Everyone takes the opportunity to hit the bars and enjoy a good beer.

Marche du Nain Rouge: Celebrated on the Sunday following the spring equinox. According to legend, Antoine de la Mothe Cadillac, Detroit's founder, was warned that he should flatter an evil creature to avoid misfortune. Unfortunately, instead of showing respect he struck the Red Dwarf and triggered his own downfall. Each year, residents march to drive this evil spirit out of the city.

Movement Festival (2): During Memorial Day weekend (late May), this major techno and electronic music festival attracts thousands of people from around the world to dance for three days, with numerous after-parties throughout the city.

© CHARLES FALSETTI

© CHARLES FALSETTI

WON'T WANT TO MISS

Hamtramck Labor Day Festival: During Labor Day weekend, a festival is held in Detroit's enclave Hamtramck, in the Polish neighborhood, featuring concerts, food stands, boat races, and wrestling matches.

Cinco de Mayo (in Southwest) (3): In the Mexican neighborhood, Cinco de Mayo commemorates the May 5, 1862 victory of General Ignacio Zaragoza over Mexican conservative troops and the French army during the Battle of Puebla.

Detroit Jazz Festival: In Downtown, at the end of August, jazz lovers can enjoy many high-quality concerts for free throughout an entire weekend.

Tec-Troit: A free electronic music festival organized every year in August. Entirely run by volunteers, it showcases local techno and house artists at the Container Globe.

Woodward Dream Cruise (4): On the third Saturday of August, the most beautiful classic cars parade down Woodward Avenue, the city's main artery, for several days to honor the Motor City.

MANY THANKS TO

To my Polish ancestors, the Chronowskis, who arrived in Detroit at the end of the 19th century, and who remain anchored in my memory throughout this American adventure.

To my friends in Core City (Chelsea, Dave, Milo, Arad, Elana, Philip, Roni, Randy, Seamus, Morgan, Shuffy, Sylvester, Victor, Darwin, Chano, Lady Worthy, William), the neighborhood that welcomed me, offered me the chance to build my home, and allows us to breathe new life into Detroit through all our beautiful projects.

To Haley, Ryan and Patrick, for all our adventures ... on bikes, by the river, at the club, at restaurants, in cars ...

To Thomas, who agreed to publish a book about Detroit, a city too little known yet so unique.

To my father, for instilling in me a love of writing since childhood.

To my mother, for giving me a taste for adventure and for sharing her childhood memories of Detroit.

To Margot and Fantine, my French friends, who support me in everything I do, encourage me, and have always believed in me.

To Sergio.

To Detroit.

This book was created by:
Margot Guicheteau, author
Olivia Fuller, translation
Jana Gough, editing
Susan R. Pollack, proofreading
Emmanuelle Willard Toulemonde, layout
Mado de La Quintinie, publishing

Cover: © Adobe Stock – Sean Pavone
Backcover and map: © H. Miller Ink

You can write to us at info@editionsjonglez.com
Follow us on Instagram: @editionsjonglez

THANKS

From the same publisher

Photo Books

Abandoned America: The age of Consequences
Abandoned Asylums
Abandoned Australia
Abandoned Belgium
Abandoned Churches: Unclaimed Places of Workship
Abandoned Cinemas of the World
Abandoned France
Abandoned Germany
Abandoned Lebanon
Abandoned Italy
Abandoned Japan
Abandoned Spain
Abandoned USSR
Abandoned World - An AI-generated exploration
After the Final Curtain: The Fall of the American Movie Theater
After the Final Curtain: America's Abandoned Theaters
Baikonur - Vestiges of the Soviet Space Program
Cinemas - A French Heritage
Chernobyl's Atomic Legacy - 25 years after disaster
Clickbait - A visual journey through AI-generated stories
Destination: Wellness - Our 35 best places in the world to make a pause
Forbidden Places - Exploring our Abandoned Heritage
Forbidden France
Forgotten Heritage
Private Islands for Rent
Oblivion
Secret Sacred Sites
Unusual Hotels Europe
Unusual Hotels - World
Unusual Hotels UK & Ireland
Unusual Nights in Paris
Unusual Shopping in Paris
Unusual Wines
Venice deserted

'Soul of' Guides

Soul of Amsterdam - A guide to the 30 best experiences
Soul of Athens - A guide to 30 exceptional experiences
Soul of Barcelona - 30 experiences
Soul of Berlin - A guide to the 30 best experiences
Soul of Brussels - A guide to exceptional experiences
Soul of Kyoto - A guide to 30 exceptional experiences
Soul of Lisbon - A guide to exceptional experiences
Soul of Los Angeles - A guide to 30 exceptional experiences
Soul of Marrakesh - A guide to 30 exceptional experiences
Soul of Marseille - A guide to exceptional experiences
Soul of Milan - A guide to exceptional experiences
Soul of New York - A guide to 30 exceptional experiences
Soul of Paris - 30 experiences
Soul of Rome - A guide to exceptional experiences
Soul of Tokyo - A guide to exceptional experiences
Soul of Venice - A guide to 30 exceptional experiences

Atlas

Atlas of forbidden places
Atlas of geographical curiosities
Atlas of extreme weather
Atlas of unusual wines

'Secret' Guides

Secret Amsterdam
Secret Bali - An unusual guide
Secret Bangkok
Secret Barcelona
Secret Bars & Restaurants in Paris
Secret Bath - An unusual guide
Secret Belfast
Secret Berlin
Secret Boston - An unusual guide
Secret Brighton - An unusual guide
Secret Brooklyn
Secret Brussels
Secret Budapest
Secret Buenos Aires
Secret Campania
Secret Cape Town
Secret Copenhagen
Secret Corsica
Secret Dolomites
Secret Dublin - An unusual guide
Secret Edinburgh - An unusual guide
Secret Florence
Secret French Riviera
Secret Geneva
Secret Glasgow
Secret Granada
Secret Helsinki
Secret Istanbul
Secret Johannesburg
Secret Lisbon
Secret Liverpool - An unusual guide
Secret London - An unusual guide
Secret London - Unusual Bars & Restaurants
Secret Los Angeles - An unusual guide
Secret Louisiana
Secret Madrid
Secret Mexico City
Secret Milan
Secret Montreal - An unusual guide
Secret Naples
Secret New Orleans - An unusual guide
Secret New York - An unusual guide
Secret New York - Curious Activities
Secret New York - Hidden Bars & Restaurants
Secret Normandy
Secret Paris
Secret Potsdam
Secret Prague
Secret Provence
Secret Rio
Secret Rome
Secret Seville
Secret Singapore
Secret Stockholm
Secret Sussex - An unusual guide
Secret Tokyo
Secret Tuscany
Secret Venice
Secret Vienna
Secret Washington DC - An unusual guide

Follow us on Facebook and Instagram

Registration of copyright: July 2025 – Edition: 01
ISBN: 978-2-36195-852-7
Printed in Bulgaria by Dedrax